Anxiety In Relationships

The Ultimate Beginners Guide to Anxiety in Relationships

By *Logan Thomas*

I0135223

EFFINGO
Publishing

For more great books, visit:

EffingoPublishing.com

Download another book for Free

We want to thank you for purchasing this book and offer you another book (just as long and valuable as this book), "Health & Fitness Mistakes You Don't Know You're Making", completely free.

Visit the link below to signup and receive it:

www.effingopublishing.com/gift

In this book, we will break down the most common health & fitness mistakes, you are probably committing right now, and will reveal how you can easily get in the best shape of your life!

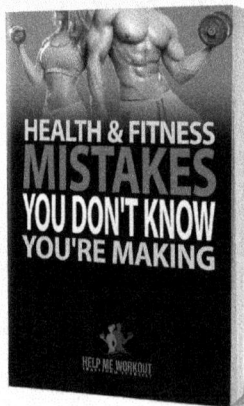

In addition to this valuable gift, you will also have an opportunity to get our new books for free, enter giveaways, and receive other valuable emails from us. Again, visit the link to sign up:

www.effingopublishing.com/gift

TABLE OF CONTENTS

INTRODUCTION

Being involved with somebody who has uneasiness or a tension issue can be very distressing. The individual's agitation can feel like an additional individual in the relationship. An irritating substance that pushed among you and your accomplice. The tension appears always to push uncertainty and disarray in the relationship. No one is set up for this in a relationship; however, you can't pick who you love, and there are no classes you can take to all the more likely set you up for adoring somebody with a psychological health issue.

However, that tension doesn't need to obliterate or put weight on a relationship. When an individual learns to understand anxiety and how it can influence the two partners and the relationship in general, the relationship can be recuperated — allowing the two partners to interface all the more profoundly on an emotional level.

This book is an informative guide on what an individual has to know whether they suffer from anxiety or in a relationship with somebody who has an anxiety issue. It will take you through the procedure of how to take out the other individual in your relationship.

Before we investigate the complexities of anxiety in a relationship, it is essential to know about what anxiety is. Anxiety can be characterized as;

The natural transformative predator/prey reaction all creatures have. Fundamentally this means in the previous days present-day progress; these were essential organic reactions that empowered individuals to dodge dangerous or savage circumstances. The peril reaction caused a surge of adrenaline, setting off a hormonal and concoction response in mind to invigorate the battle or flight reaction. This readies the body to face a circumstance or escape to well-being physically. In an advanced society, these reactions are currently activated by pressure brought about by work, cash deficiencies, well-being concerns, and others consistently saw dangers to our prosperity. It is usually depicted as a sentiment of nerves or butterflies or insecurity and is simply an appearance of our single battle or flight reaction.

Uneasiness issues, albeit still a piece of the average organic capacity, happen when there is an unbalanced response to unpleasant boosts. These unbalanced responses cause a physical reaction that goes on for a more extended than an ordinary period and incorporate uplifted circulatory strain, sweating, shaking, queasiness, and a need to confine oneself. Further to this present, the sufferer's from a tension issue may intuitively show thoughts and situations that trigger further battle or flight reactions. These reactions typically render the nervousness sufferer unequipped for working on an everyday premise as they circle unendingly all through tension.

Discovering that your partner has tension can happen either when they let you know or when you find out through their conduct. It is never simple to concede an individual has a psychological issue, so talking about your partner's anxiety ought to be handled sensitively. Regardless of whether you are telling your partner that you experience the ill effects of tension, or getting some information about their nervousness, how the subject is discussed can represent the moment of truth a relationship. Here are a few things to remember while talking about anxiety in a relationship;

• Anxiety can't be decreased; it is a real issue and isn't something individuals compensate for consideration. Uneasiness is a psychological well-being issue.

• Anxiety is an ordinary human reaction, and everybody has it now and again. Anguish possibly turns into a problem or confusion on the off chance that it gets severe and enduring.

• Anxiety can be damaging to an individual and can keep individuals from jumping on throughout everyday life or in any event, working accurately.

- Anxiety can make individuals experience their daily battle or-flight reaction to things that are not dangerous. This can incorporate unreasonable stress over if their accomplice is cheating or making arrangements to leave them.

- Anxiety can't be fixed or relieved.

- People who experience the ill effects of nervousness don't need it. As a rule, they stress over whether they are a weight to the individuals around them or their loved ones.

- Around the world, a massive number of individuals experience the ill effects of nervousness. In spite of this, they have upbeat, sound connections that flourish.

- Anxiety can come in waves that are reliable or sporadic. Those experiencing nervousness issues have quieted in their side effects, where uneasiness doesn't influence them by any stretch of the imagination.

- Logic and discerning are unrealistic when experiencing tension. Individuals who have uneasiness stress over things regardless of whether they can't be demonstrated. This implies the pressure will make them think unreasonably and without rationale. Most occasions, their accomplice thinks about the sufferer's considerations.

- You are not feeble on the off chance that you experience the ill effects of tension.

- Anxiety can be dealt with. With treatment and home, practice tension can be soothed as the uneasiness sufferer figures out how to the arrangement and adapt to their side effects.

- If you experience the ill effects of uneasiness, odds are you invest a great deal of energy stressing and brainstorming situations where things turn out badly or end up contrarily. Individuals with tension frequently over break down connections. They pose inquiries that must be replied with negative answers which affirm their considerations.

These inquiries in some cases resemble this;

- What if he/she doesn't cherish me as much as I love him?

- What is the fact that he/she is misleading me?

- What is the fact that he/she is concealing something from me?

- What if he/she is undermining me?

- What if he/she needs to threaten me?

- What if he/she loves another person better?

- What if my uneasiness ruins our relationship? (this is called nervousness about the anguish)

- What on the off chance that we separate?

- What if he/she doesn't content me back?

- What in case I'm generally the first to connect?

- What on the off chance that he/she doesn't pitch when they are going to me?

While it is typical for individuals to have these sorts of thoughts and inquiries now and then, anxiety amplifies them. Those with a nervousness issue consider these inquiries frequently and with intensity. People with nervousness imagine the worst-case scenario, enabling their brains to assume control over their balanced manner of thinking. Anxious thoughts can cause physiological side effects in the body. These side effects include;

- Breath Shortness

- Insomnia

- Attacks of Anxiety

- Fight Responses

Nervousness doesn't just influence the individual experiencing it. It can put anxiety on your partner and can devastate a relationship. A prime case of this is when individuals with anxiety attempt to test their partner's level of commitment by using insecure strategies. In this situation, the anxiety sufferer is having though about them being the person who always starts the communication. The individual with nervousness begins to stress that their partner never again prefers them in the manner they used to because he/she isn't the first to communicate as regularly as the sufferer does. The tension at that point develops, and the individual with anxiety begins to accept that their partner will never interact with them if they don't text them first. While trying to fix their nervousness, the individual chooses to ignore their partner for a small period. This powers their partner to be the first to communicate until the sufferer starts to feel much improved, realizing that their partner is attempting to talk. These facts show that their anxiety is irrational as their partner did initiate contact. The issue is, this is not an excellent way to address anxiety.

Sadly, anxiety conduct can manifest in many different in a relationship. Practically every one of them is undesirable.

These practices can be;

- Being furious, peevish

- Being controlling

- Being diverted and experiencing difficulty centering

- Coming crosswise over as excessively basic

- Avoidant or inactive forceful conduct

- Perfectionism

Tension, whenever left unchecked, can have final results on your physical well-being as well. Other than the ordinary physical reactions related to stress, progressing and extreme uneasiness can cause;

- Suppression of the insusceptible framework

- Digestive issues and interminable issue

- Acute solid strain

- Elevated circulatory strain

- Short term memory misfortune

- Coronary vein illness

- Heart assaults and stroke

These physical issues can be devastating if anxiety isn't overseen in a proper manner. To cope with the constraints attached to being in a relationship, one must show patience. This mostly leads to anxiety. You, as a person who has just been into a relationship, must abide by the fact that things never go one-sided. One must show flexibility to work things around. If not, then anxiety is waiting for you, which never leads to a good lasting relationship and even effects your capabilities of performing daily routine workload, and one may suffer health issues.

The chapters underneath will help you as the nervousness sufferer to manage your anxiety productively. I am helping you and your partner to work through your mental and health and strengthen your relationship.

Also, before you get started, I recommend you **joining our email newsletter** to receive updates on any upcoming new book releases or promotions. You can sign-up for free, and as a bonus, you will receive a gift. Our *"Health & Fitness Mistakes You Don't Know You're Making"* book! This book has been written to demystify, expose the top do's and don'ts and to finally equip you with the information you need to get in the best shape of your life. Due to the overwhelming amount of misinformation and lies told by magazines and self-proclaimed "gurus," it's becoming harder and harder to get reliable information to get in shape. As opposed to having to go through dozens of biased, unreliable, and untrustworthy sources to get your health & fitness information. Everything you need to help you has been broken down in this book for you to easily follow and to immediately get results to achieve your desired fitness goals in the shortest amount of time.

Once again, to join our free email newsletter and to receive a free copy of this valuable book, please visit the link and sign-up now on: **www.effingopublishing.com/gift.**

Chapter 1: Conquer Your Emotions

Anxiety doesn't have to risk your relationship. At the point when you conquer your feelings and utilize the correct adapting strategies, you can have a stable relationship. These adapting strategies will prevent anxiety from causing stress on your relationship.

The kind of thinking that leads to emotional weakness regularly begins in adolescence. We depend on our parents for all our enthusiastic needs – love, comfort, approval, and so on. Also, along these lines, we don't regularly wholly build up the abilities to freely bolster our passionate quality as youngsters, because our parents, out of love, do their best to provide for all our needs.

At the point when you are dating someone, it is easy to fall into the trap of using them as a substitute therapist. Your partner isn't your therapist. However, they ought not to be playing that kind of role. By expecting them to be your therapist, you are opening them up to become emotionally attached. This could prompt hatred from your partner. Ultimately it isn't your partner's duty to provide you free therapy. The task regarding taking control of your emotions lies with you as the anxiety sufferer. You are seeing a specialist who can show you substantial ways of dealing with stress that will improve your satisfaction in and outside of your relationship. On the off chance that you are in a long submitted relationship, you may consider heading off to a couple's sessions to work through any nervousness gives that are based on your relationship. By doing this, you are easing the pressure off of your partner and your relationship.

Try not to be disheartened if your partner opposes from the start; keep on going to treatment without anyone else. It will assist you with building up your adapting skills and will help you with bettering impart your anxiety to your partner. By dealing with your very own psychological well-being, you are on the correct way to assuming responsibility for your feelings.

Why Negative Thinking is Toxic

Negative thinking is very harmful! It puts a damper on an individual's eagerness and inspiration both in and outside of their relationship. Negative thinking adds to hesitation, dawdling, dormancy, and wrecking of one's objectives and achievement. Negative musings rout you and have you crying that your life is full of misfortune. In any case, the fact of the matter is your negative thoughts make you the cause of all your problems. At the point when you enable yourself to enjoy negative feelings, you are making your very own misfortune. These negative thoughts can be;

- It won't work out

- I'm unfortunate

- Something will undoubtedly turn out badly

- My accomplice is hopeless

- Why trouble

- I cannot do this

There truly is a constant measure of negative messages in fluctuating shapes and sizes that you can let yourself know. These dishearten you from being proactive and pushing ahead in your relationship. To break the cycle, you should quit enabling negative thoughts to enter your psyche in this manner giving them control.

Generally, you have gotten so used to your very own negative reasoning that you aren't even mindful of the way that you are doing it anymore. This is a significant issue! You have to turn out to be increasingly aware again. When you can perceive the negative words and considerations, you can stop and counter them with positive or alternate messages. By being sure and hopeful, you can transform negativity into truth, not fear. Because things haven't turned out in different connections or you have been disillusioned in the past doesn't imply that they won't be diverse this time. You are the master of your destiny, and when you change negativity to inspire all of you, your hopeful outlook to shine through into your relationship.

On a subconscious level, your negativity is a defense mechanism that shields you from anything terrible that could happen, which could hurt you emotionally. By accepting your association with negativity, you think you are mellowing the blow if your relationship comes up short. In reality, you are just ruining your relationship. The nervousness and anticipation of the relationship failing contribute to blocking any happiness and inspiration from entering the relationship. It stops the flow of positive energy and creates stress on your partner.

A healthy mind requires various fruits of positivity, compassion, and understanding. Likewise, appreciating and respecting the differences of your partner is one golden rule that binds people. Financial independence, if given to a person, enhances one's emotional health and creates a sense of compassion. Negative thoughts can eventually serve as a relationship killer. There exists a feedback loop between a person's thoughts, behaviors, and feelings. In this way, negative thinking is a form of self-abuse. Thus passive thinking can sabotage a relationship. To overcome this chronic negativity, a person should be willing to practice mindfulness and acknowledge the partner's positive accomplishment. Sometimes our mind works through distortion, i.e., we assume the inaccurate thoughts to be accurate and in result, assume the worst possible outcome. The best way to overcome this negativity is that we must be ready to release judgment. We shouldn't be comparing our lives to many unrealistic situations that only cause us discomfort. Whenever you notice any negativity in your partner, look for a positive quality too. Its human nature to dwell on pessimistic sides of people rather than focusing on strengths. But always remember that optimism is a gem. Just distract yourself towards something fun and productive.

At the point when you let dread and negativity crash you, you are subconsciously ruining your relationship, instead of expecting the worst terrible from your partner attempt to imagine the best. You can even now reveal to yourself that the link may not work, yet you need to talk about your issues with your partner. Negativity is very harmful to a relationship. Figure out how to act naturally mindful and positive with yourself, and at last, you will start to feel increasingly associated with your partner.

Jealousy; Being Consumed by Your Emotions

Nobody appreciates feeling jealous or consumed by jealousy. Even though jealousy is an unavoidable feeling that nearly everybody encounters from time to time, jealousy that devours inner of you is very devastating. Jealousy can take control over your life on the off chance that you don't get a grip on it, and it can overwhelm you. It can be very harmful and can destroy a relationship. At the point when you allow jealousy to overwhelm you or your partner, you are potentially ruining your very own relationship. By attempting to understand where your jealous sentiments are originating from, figuring out how to manage them, and discovering approaches to adjust to your feelings, you are allowing your relationship to prosper.

So what is this jealousy is?

Studies have indicated that jealousy goes hand in hand with low self-esteem. Numerous individuals are unaware of the way that disgrace is a part of anxiety. It goes hand in hand with negative and self-created musings. For the individuals who experience the ill effects of nervousness, disgrace can vigorously impact how jealous or uncertain they feel.

Basic, negative considerations sustain dangerous practices and emotions, driving you to analyze, pass judgment, and assess yourself against others. For tension sufferers, this assessment is finished with extraordinary examination and obsessiveness. These basic, negative thoughts will, in general, fuel envy and feed suspicious interior discussions. Jealousy in anxiety is usually established in previous experience, maybe a separation, a partner who cheated from somebody you once loved.

In a relationship, jealousy wrecks cherishing, understanding relationship. The more you clutch sentiments of resentment, the more you will find in general drive a wedge among you. Dividing that you are so unnerved of occurring. Remember, jealousy frequently originates from sentiments of weakness or disgrace in ourselves. These negative, jealous emotions become anxious thoughts that can sound like the following;

She wouldn't like to associate with you

- There must be another person.

- He's losing interest.

- My accomplice is hopeless.

- He needs to escape from you.

- Who would need to hear you out?

- You're so exhausting

The individuals who experience the ill effects of anxiety know about these considerations experiencing our brains; however, jealousy starts to frame when these structures begin to get over the top. The main problem comes in that those with uneasiness will, in general, retreat trying to shield themselves from the envisioned threat or pain that they believe is happening. Be that as it may, the more you retreat, the further removed your partner will become, and the more jealous you are going to be. By effectively taking a shot at your nervousness and your envious emotions, you are making your relationship a need and deciding to love and close with your partner rather than desirous and insecure. By using the tools below and further along in this book, you will have the option to all the more likely deal with your desire;

1.   **Know what is activating you.** Would it be that makes your nervousness mix? Are there explicit occasions or individuals? Maybe it is a companion who is faithful or an ex/sweetheart that is present with another person. Possibly it is a colleague who is by all accounts improving at their specific employment?

2. Identify your basic internal voice and when it begins to gab. Attempt to recognize what considerations make you feel envious. Is it true that you are just jealous, or are your considerations pulling you down and making you scrutinize yourself? It is safe to say that you are feeling irrelevant or not fit for progress as a result of them? Do your musings come in waves that have a particular patter or feel to them?

3. What are the ramifications of your musings, and where do they come from? Are your considerations making you feel strain to accomplish or be something you are not? Do you have a feeling that you ought to resemble another person? If you changed, would it be a positive change? Is your envy established from quite a while ago?

Precisely how would you manage desire? Going to treatment will deal with your emotions in a positive manner that instructs you are adapting aptitudes. By utilizing the focuses underneath you will likewise be better prepared to excuse your envy and work through it;

- **Think about what is causing your desire** – You can think about what sentiments, individuals, and sensations cause you to get desirous and flood your brain with envious musings. Is what you are feeling connected to a past occasion? Maybe it a family relationship or a current negative observation from your youth. When you can associate your feelings and overcompensations to the things that occurred in your past, you will have a more transparent way on the most proficient method to work through those sentiments in the present.

• **Remain powerless and remain quiet in the present** – I don't make a difference in how desirous you are; there is continuously an approach to discover your way back to your actual self and to mollify your standpoint. This should be possible by tolerating that you are human and by managing your very own sentiments humanely. Recall that desire and tension goes back and forth in waves; they will steadily assemble and die down after some time. You can acknowledge your envy and recognize your emotions without responding to it and learning apparatuses that assist you with working through your desire without overcompensating. Mitigating breaths and long strolls are only a portion of the procedures that will help you with calming yourself. Recall that it is simpler to quiet down when you don't endure or tune in to the negative words and contemplations that originate from your internal pundit. Picking up quieting strategies can be troublesome; however, it is a fundamental instrument to assist you with facing your very own essential contemplations. By doing this, you can get defenseless and open to those that you love and care for, fortifying your relationship.

•   **Stop carrying on** – The inward voice that makes you blow up and guide you to lash out at your accomplice and companions causes long haul harm in your connections. On the off chance that you enable it to wind crazy and you are stuck in a look of desire, it might even devastate your relationship altogether. This is a type of self-harm because the willingness makes you lash out or rebuff somebody you care for without it being their shortcoming. This is particularly valid for individuals in a relationship. At the point when you do this, you are making the very situation you are generally terrified of. You may wind up harming and undermining your accomplice, which affronts their adoration for you. This like this will exacerbate your very own sentiments of doubt and the dread that they will leave you. Indeed, you may accidentally urge them to follow up on your conduct, making them become shut off from you, concealing their emotions or their activities to maintain a strategic distance from your doubt and desire.

- **Find security in yourself** – Focusing on yourself and finding your very own feeling of self-security is the best thing you can accomplish for sentiments of envy that trigger nervousness. It may not be simple yet by taking every necessary step to quietness the pundit inside you and persuade yourself that you will be alright, regardless of whether that implies being without anyone else is fundamental. The acknowledgment that you needn't bother with one explicit individual to cherish you to entire and cheerful is enabling. Individuals are normally defective and have constraints, and understanding that one individual can't give you everything that you need constantly is significant. At the point when you practice empathy with yourself, you can face the basic voice inside and your negative considerations. You don't have to close individuals out or disengage yourself from the world to have the option to be sympathetic to yourself. What is means that you grasp your life, your defects, and your weaknesses totally, realizing that you are sufficiently able to defeat challenges and disappointments. Recall that the main thing you can control in life is how you respond to your conditions. Decide to respond entirely.

- **Don't quit being focused** – While a few people don't care for being aggressive, it is excellent whenever done accurately. Being focused doesn't mean you are deciding to be the best at something. It implies you can set a reasonable objective and state that you are giving your best to have the option to accomplish it. At the point when you are focused on yourself, you are grasping everything that will assist you with positively achieving your objectives. Rather than being envious, negative, and lashing out, you can rouse yourself and associate with the best characteristics in you. When you have associated with your internal identity, you will have the option to find a way to carry you closer to your objectives. Regard is earned, not consequently offered, and to gain that regard; you should be thoughtful in your activities and aware of the ramifications for those activities. In like manner, on the off chance that you need to feel adored and acknowledged reliably by your accomplice, you should be willing to being cherishing and make them feel esteemed in your relationship as well. When you are reliable in your need to act with uprightness and to effectively seek after your objectives, you can win the fight against uneasiness that is brought about by desire and begin to become yourself again — somebody who is isolated from any other individual and one of a kind.

- **Don't avoid discussing it** – When desire starts to assume control over, it gets significant for you to locate the correct individual to discuss your emotions in a manner that is sound for you to express precisely how you feel. These individuals are the ones who bolster your positive characteristics and who help you not to become mixed up in your negative contemplations or spiraling into envy. Everybody has companions who blow up or get stirred up when specific themes are examined, and we are not saying they shouldn't be your companions. However, they are not the individuals you should converse with when you feel envious or restless. These individuals will most likely make you feel increasingly anxious or desirous before the finish of the discussion. Due to this, you should search out individuals who won't just help you yet will assist you with thinking sanely about the circumstance. At the point when you are addressing these individuals, make sure to recognize to yourself that your negative musings are unreasonable and that your sentiments are not right. This causes you to alleviate feelings of desire because the sounding load up enables you to listen to your musings boisterous, helping you to change your activities and how you would respond. If excitement turns out to be an excess of you should discover help from a specialist who can assist you with understanding how you are feeling, how to deal with those sentiments, and work through the foundation of where your feelings of envy are originating from.

Jealousy is an inevitable emotion that lives within us all. We all experience it from time to time. It is frightening to see how this emotion influences a person when they let it over-power them. The voice of jealousy arises from suspicious commentary in our heads, and with time it's even harder to cope. Our jealousy may be a romantic or competitive one. But no matter how jealous a person may feel, but he must be ready to soften. Our inner voice advises us to immediately act and take action that can cause hurt in the long run. But we need to understand that we don't always need the love of one person to make us feel overwhelmed. We need to keep our feeling healthier, which allow us to give space to our partner.

Connection; Determining Success and Failure

Your style of connection can straightforwardly influence your determination of an accomplice to how your relationship advances or how they end. Perceiving your connection example can enable you to comprehend what your qualities and shortcomings are seeing someone. Connection designs are generally framed at an early stage in your adolescence and keep on working as the working model for how you create connections as a grown-up. Your connection model impacts how you respond to your needs and how you approach having them satisfied. Constructive secure connections happen when an individual is sure and mindful. These individuals usually are ready to connect effectively with others and can address their accomplice's issues without issues or envy. A restless connection design ordinarily prompts nervousness or separation happening in the relationship as the sufferer remembers their youth design.

Safely connected grown-ups will, in general, be progressively fulfilled in their connections. Kids with a safe connection consider there to be a protected base from which they can wander out and freely investigate the world. A safe grown-up has a comparative association with their sentimental accomplice, having a sense of safety and associated while enabling themselves and their accomplice to move unreservedly.

Secure grown-ups offer help when their accomplice feels troubled. They likewise go to their accomplices for comfort when they feel pained. Their relationship will, in general, be straightforward, open, and equivalent, with the two individuals, feeling autonomous yet cherishing toward one another.

In contrast to safely connected couples, individuals with an on-edge connection will, in general, be urgent to frame a dream bond with theirs. Rather than feeling genuine love or trust toward their accomplice, they frequently think passionate appetite. They are now and again looking to their accomplice to protect or finish them. Even though they are looking for a feeling of well-being and security by sticking to their accomplice, they take activities that push their accomplice away always, regardless of whether deliberately or sub intentionally.

Even though restlessly connected people act urgent or unreliable, usually, their conduct compounds their very own feelings of trepidation. At the point when they feel uncertain of their accomplice's emotions and dangerous in their relationship, they regularly become tenacious, requesting, or possessive toward their accomplice. They may likewise translate free activities by their accomplice as confirmation of their feelings of dread when, actually, their accomplice's conduct has nothing to do with their musings. For instance, if their accomplice begins mingling more with companions, they may think, "See? He doesn't generally cherish me. He would prefer to invest energy with his companions. This implies he is going to leave me. I was correct not to confide in him."

Individuals with a pompous avoidant connection tend to remove themselves from their accomplices sincerely. They may look for separation and feel pseudo-free, assuming the job of child-rearing their accomplice themselves. They regularly appear to be centered around themselves and might be excessively mindful of their everyday luxuries.

Dreadful Avoidant Attachment – An individual with a frightful avoidant connection lives in a conflicted state, in which they fear to be both excessively near or excessively far off from others. They attempt to keep their sentiments under control however are not ready to. They can't only stay away from their nervousness or flee from their emotions. Instead, they are overpowered by their responses and regularly experience enthusiastic tempests. They will, in general, be stirred up or erratic in their dispositions. They see their connections from the working model that they have defined in their minds and look towards others to get their needs met, yet in the event that they draw near to other people, they will hurt you. As it were, the individual they need to go to for security is a similar individual. They are startled to be near. Therefore, they have no sorted out the procedure for getting their needs met by others.

As grown-ups, these people will, in general, end up in rough or emotional connections, with numerous highs and lows. They regularly have fears of being deserted yet, in addition, battle with being close. They may stick to their accomplice when they feel dismissed, at that point, contact caught when they are close. Customarily, the planning is by all accounts off among them and their accomplices. An individual with a dreadful avoidant connection may even end up in a harsh relationship.

You can challenge your safeguard components by picking join forces with a protected connection style and work on creating yourself in that relationship. Treatment can likewise be useful for changing wrong connection designs. By getting mindful of your connection style, both you and your accomplice can challenge the instabilities and fears bolstered by your deep-rooted working models and grow new styles of connection for continuing an excellent, cherishing relationship.

Insecurity as a sign of weakness

It isn't unexpected to encounter uncertainty now and again in a romantic relationship. Everybody sooner or later in their relationship has addressed whether their accomplice is the ideal individual for them. As per insights, around 40% of individuals have felt unreliable about their relationship sooner or later or the other. In a relationship, however, individuals who have a sense of safety have fewer issues and are more joyful than the individuals who are uncertain. This is because secure individuals are better ready to help their accomplice in the relationship.

We have just settled that negative thoughts can fuel other more noteworthy issues. One of these issues is an absence of passionate certainty and security. Believing that your accomplice won't undermine you doesn't imply that you don't feel insecure. Coming up next are signs that you are unreliable and may need to make a move to address your conduct before it starts to influence your relationship;

• **You Don't Trust Easily** - You question each seemingly insignificant detail, you stalk online networking locales, you snoop on your accomplice, or you feel compromised effectively.

• **You Need Reassurance to Feel Secure** - You question each seemingly insignificant detail, you stalk web based life destinations, you snoop on your accomplice, or you feel compromised effectively.

• **You Become Panicked Easily** - During a contention, you alarm that your accomplice will leave, will dismiss you, or may pass judgment on you.

• **You Easily Feel Attacked** - You feel promptly insulted, hurt, or shut somewhere near something your accomplice asks of you, you in a split second feel scrutinized and need to safeguard yourself by belligerence or by closing down totally.

- **You Don't Accept Yourself** - You battle with regards to giving yourself consent to be you, you judge yourself regularly and hold yourself to particular requirements.

- **You Create Mountains Over Molehills** - You start ruckuses and make them outrageous issues, you utilize terrible or complete words and make enormous contentions around something that isn't large once you've made a stride back.

- **You Struggle with Intimacy** – When you battle with feeling near your accomplice both genuinely and explicitly, and you can feel your watchman going up during personal minutes.

So how would you right your conduct and getting secure in yourself and your relationship once more?

Practice care and expound on how or why you feel how you do. Inquire as to whether you can challenge your contemplations and assume the best about your accomplice.

At the point when you get physically involved with your partner, ask yourself whether you and your partner experience closeness and intimacy similarly. Then work on why you are putting up your guard. Once you have established why you are putting your guard up, practice, and put into place ways in which you can be vulnerable with your partner. Recall that being powerless doesn't mean being feeble. What it does is assemble a solid bond with your adored one where you are giving them that you confide in them profoundly.

Recognize the first occasion when you felt this feeling of frenzy and pinpoint it to an opportunity to perceive how it's assuming a job in your present circumstance. What did you have to hear at that point, and what do you have to understand now? On the off chance that it's merely the equivalent, take a stab at advising that message when you begin to feel activated once more. Presently ask yourself these inquiries: "What number of my considerations are suspicions?" "What did my accomplice state?" "Can there be a probability I'm disguising this situation and making it something it's not?" Reflect on three to five battles you've had previously and take a gander at them objectively.

Attachment is one cruel disease that is an unhealthy fruit for relationships. An over-attached person creates a sense of insecurity, but in the same way, attachment, if dealt with care, can do wonders. For relationship beginners, when you freely communicate and deliberately speak your heart out, you get used to it. And as time passes, the feeling of not getting to know everything makes one insecure.

Embracing Resolutions; Reducing Conflict

The most well-known instances of a relationship in a difficult situation is how the partner differ or battle with one another and how they settle the matter between them. Their goals whether negative or positive can influence the tone of the relationship and how clashes are dealt with later on. Contradictions that form into petty squabbling or restless steady clash, as a rule, end up in a more uncertain possibility of the relationship enduring. Couples who go to treatment as a rule do it to help their relationship in healing. Treatment stops negative associations between the two and acquires positive correspondence.

It is usual for individuals in a relationship to need to feature the positive parts of their relationship and to need to overlook the awful ones. Couples love one another, and on account of this, they tend to forgive and never revisit trusting that the eventual fate of their relationship will be better. However, when negative examples return in a relationship, the harm begins to become irreparable.

By looking for treatment, couples can stop damaging clashes before they start to wreck the relationship. Research done shows that partners who are ceaselessly contending or experience no success clashes are concealing further issues inside. These issues should be fixed all together for the relationship to become stable once more. This is particularly apparent in couples who quarrel over things that can't or won't unite them. When couples see that the battle is impossible to win the fight and stop effectively captivating in them, they become familiar with the aptitudes to interface viably. This mends their relationship and enables the two accomplices to recover love and trust in one another.

With regards to nervousness in a relationship, one partner urgently needs sustaining, absolution, or backing while the other may feel furious, angry, or inaccessible. For the individual with tension, this fills in as affirmation of their dread and their sentiments of dismissal regardless of how hard they attempt to reject their accomplice's conduct. The issue with uneasiness is that it is regularly the tension sufferer who makes their accomplices sentiments of hatred and outrage through their behavior. Unfortunately, tension makes conduct where the sufferer frequently winds up harvesting what they sew with their accomplice turning out to be increasingly more far off after some time.

Conflict is a visible sign that a relationship between two people needs to grow. Tense battles lead to chaos and discomfort. Whenever a person has a strong urge to win every argument, that is when conflicts arise. But there is always a right way to win every situation. Relationships survive when both people make an effort to battle conflict rather than the blame game. Not speaking or being angry towards your partner is when silence begins to overshadow a relationship. It builds resentment and makes the other person feel punished and confused. To resolve this, two people need to be open to what they want from each other. They should always be ready to listen without judgment. Constant mean words can also tear your partner's moral. Therefore, choose your words wisely. Ever let go of the baggage of past. Reminiscing the old mistakes is just pointless. You can only take care of your relationship if only you take care of yourself first.

Reconnecting with Your Partner Emotionally

At the point when your relationship first starts, they are energizing and exciting. For a few, anxiety doesn't sneak in until some other time, when the connection has created. Shockingly, however, for individuals who experience the ill effects of nervousness, sooner or later, it will raise its head, taking steps to demolish the relationship.

At the point when tension assumes control over a relationship, frequently, the partner feels neglected or angry and may begin to get far off. By reconnecting sincerely with your partner, you can construct a more grounded relationship. With a more grounded relationship, nervousness should start to reduce, and it will enable your relationship to develop into a solid association.

So how would you approach reconnecting with your partner a passionate level?

Initially, you have to recognize that your tension is most likely an enormous part of why you and your partner feel disengaged from one another. By understanding your conduct, regardless of whether deliberate or not, on the off chance that you can discuss your uneasiness and show that you are have found a way to address your conduct.

Here are a few hints on the most proficient method to reconnect no sweat nervousness in your relationship;

Associate with your accomplice consistently; as your relationship develops, you and your accomplice will turn out to be less eager to get to know one another.

This is fine and ordinary. Toward the start of a relationship, we hang out because we need to become more acquainted with one another.

At this point, you likely know it all you have to think about your accomplice. Investing energy with them turns out to be less critical to you.

You don't know it about your accomplice.

Continue attempting to reconnect. You may have done some time back when you were always associating. Be that as it may, individuals are not static; they are continually evolving.

Your accomplice is unexpected today in comparison to they were yesterday, in simple ways.

Require significant investment consistently to invest some energy alone together, sitting idle yet speaking and looking at nothing significant.

Existing with one another separated keeps you associated such that feels more enthusiastic than down to earth.

A sense of connection is crucial for relationships. Take an interest in your partner's routine, like what they do daily. It is only the smaller things when done with love affects the other person. When we get to know someone, we also know their dark sides. But acceptance is necessary. We need to hold the other person in their positive light. People in healthy relationships connect to work out their arguments and repair quickly. No relationship is perfect, and we can always be someone that brings out the best in others. Building a good relationship still requires time and effort on both ends. This world is full of good people. If you can't find one, be one.

CHAPTER 2: CAN ANXIETY BE POSITIVE

Anxiety appears to have negative meanings; however, investigate has demonstrated that anxiety can have preferences and advantages.

An individual who experiences tension knows the extreme dread, stress, and apprehension that accompanies their anxiety. Portrayed some of the time as a consistent sentiment of apprehension or fear, anxiety can lead you to feel diverted and unattached from your partner and the outside world. The physical reactions can influence your feelings as well as can add to progressively negative emotions and thoughts.

Anxiety is a feeling that is regularly portrayed by extreme dread, stress, and worry. Numerous anxiety sufferers describe it as a sentiment of apprehension and fear that can be diverting, best case scenario, and all-consuming at worst. Anxiety is regularly experienced on numerous levels, influencing one's feelings, prompting awkward physical sensations, and adding to negative thoughts. Be that as it may, nervousness can have beneficial outcomes as well, and underneath we will investigate so of those.

A specific degree of nervousness is something to be thankful for. Research shows that high pressure can propel and energize an individual in their life. Anxiety can be only the admonition sign. You have to carry attention to your present circumstance and roll out some vital improvements throughout your life. Steady stress and anxiety can be a sign that a few aspects of your life are off track and need altering. For example, you may find that you have a relationship that is never again working, maybe your activity is causing a lot of pressure, or perhaps monetary issues make them lose rest and feeling on edge. Your manifestations can be hard to oversee, yet investigating and adapting to your anxiety can be a genuine open door for self-growth. The next time anxiety strikes, consider what message it has for you and the possible adjustments you may need to make in your life. Rather than always being considered a hindrance, anxiety may help you feel more motivated and prepared when faced with challenges. Research has shown that students and athletes who encountered some nervousness showed improved execution on tests or while taking part in aggressive games. In like manner, some level of tension in the individuals who have a decent working memory may upgrade execution on intellectual tests.

Consider ways that your nervousness makes a motivating force for you to be fruitful in certain aspects of your life. For example, maybe your anxiety helps you in placing additional exertion into work or individual undertakings, establishing a decent connection, or moving towards your objectives. While thinking about your very own nervousness, attempt to consider ways that you can utilize it for your development and personal growth. Even though it might appear to be pointless now and again, there is a reason for uneasiness. These emotions and indications are a part of our natural method for managing pressure. Known as the battle or-flight reaction, nervousness is intended to shield us from threats and enable us to respond quickly to crises. At the point when it went to our ancestors, the battle or-flight pressure reaction arranged people to either assault back or escape from a dangerous hazard in the earth, for example, a terrible creature or atmosphere condition. In present-day times, anxiety might be a symptom that causes you to rapidly respond to maintain a strategic distance from a mishap while driving a vehicle or keep you from entering a dangerous spot or situation. A study found that kids who experienced nervousness had fewer mishaps and unintentional death in early adulthood than the individuals who didn't have nervousness. In this sense, anxiety may be a sign to help keep you safe. A person who has managed tension might be progressively sympathetic and comprehension to the issues that others face. Having experienced individual battles, yourself, you might be gradually touchy, loving, and accepting when loved ones are managing personal difficulties. It's been shown that people with anxiety are more concerned about how they interact with others. Have you seen that you, at times, have all the earmarks of being only that companion somebody needs? Individuals with nervousness may likewise be gifted in influential positions, as they take cautious thought of the plausibility of many results. Your battle with tension might adversely influence your profession, connections, and individual desires.

Anxiety as a Tool to Shape Strong Personalities

The individuals who have nervousness can now and then seem to be calm, disinterested, or quiet. In all actuality, a great deal of the time you are taking on an internal conflict or taking in your surroundings before you take part in a discussion or start a significant association. This is because you are attempting to watch yourself from conceivably being harmed or dismissed.

Parties and occasions can cause a ton of uneasiness for you, and being around individuals can trigger uncertainties or fits of anxiety. For those with anxiety, coming out of their shell and showing the strength of their personality can be an uphill battle. A conscious effort should be made to put yourself out there and to talk yourself through the negative musings. Through treatment and establishing the rules in this book, it is possible though to build a strong personality even when suffering from anxiety.

A solid character doesn't mean you should be loud, intimidating, or over the top to show your personality. It is possible to have a solid role in calm certainty too. Here are a few hints and deceives to assist you with building a solid character while experiencing nervousness;

Listen before you speak

Far too often, anxiety drives us to over-respond or avoid indicating individuals what our identity is. At the point when you take part in a discussion with the expect to tune in before talking, you permit your mind, and your uneasiness time to process the data, the individual is letting you know reasonably. Once you have listened and taken in what the other person has said, you can respond. This enables you to interface with an individual on a more profound, progressively significant level and aids precisely in deciding whether you might want to keep on building an association with them. The test is that for those with anxiety, they frequently don't talk except if addressed. Given this, individuals may order you as standoffish or excessively peaceful, and on account of that, they won't address you first. To conquer this, you should have enough power over your uneasiness to begin a discussion and start to show the world your solid character. At the point when you talk first, the other individual will naturally draw in with you, and this opens you up to have the option to tune in to what they are stating. Remember to employ empathetic conversation to show that you are engaged and that the person has your attention while they are talking.

Actions speak louder than words sometimes.

Having a solid character doesn't always mean that you need to speak to be heard, and this is, in some cases, a more straightforward method to impart on the off chance that you experience the ill effects of nervousness. Being in a room or a relationship where others are stronger, more flashy may feel overpowering. Your uneasiness may leave you feeling frustrated and meaningless in these sorts of settings; however, you don't have to feel that way.

There are various online web and in-person courses that show an individual how to be self-assured and confident while never opening their mouths to talk. Figuring out how to be satisfied in your non-verbal communication, a confident handshake and an open body position can help massively when trying to portray a strong character and an eagerness to speak with others. From the outset, it will be hard not to stay away and enable your nervousness to dominate; however, the more you practice confidence, the simpler it will become to depict yourself as strong and confident.

Accept praise, where it is due.

What's more, consistently give credit when it is expected. At the point when you experience the ill effects of nervousness, you will, in general, take praises and recognition sparingly, frightened that the commendation is a hidden affront, or more terrible! That you may disappoint the person, who is complimenting you. At the point when somebody praises, you set aside the effort to tune in to what they are stating and honestly acknowledge it. Unless you know the person to be sarcastic, their praise is rooted in truth. Continuously make sure to express gratitude toward them, and here is the marginally harder part, make sure to offer credit to anybody that has helped you make your progress. For example, you are praised for a venture at work. Your reaction would be thank you so much; I don't figure it would have been anyplace close as fruitful if not for the assistance of my partner.

This tells people you are engaging, but more importantly, it says to them that you are secure enough and reliable enough in your personality to be able to accept the praise and acknowledge that you didn't do it by yourself. Individuals with solid characters and nearness are specific, and even though anxiety can strip you of that, figuring out how to acknowledge acclaim again will assist you with reconstructing your certainty — indicating individuals exactly how solid you are.

The following two points are the hardest for tension sufferers to pursue yet are essential to a solid character. Prevent looking for an endorsement from others and avoid your head. Extreme right? As you've read in this book, anxiety bases itself in negative thoughts that swirl uncontrollably in your mind, causing a psychological and physical response. These negative musings and restless sentiments drive you to look for endorsement from others as an approach to approving your feelings. At the point when you escape your very own head and break the cycle of negative considerations, you can start the act of self-approval. Mindfulness and self-esteem begin to shape, which encourages your character to form into one of solidarity and certainty. Individuals who experience the ill effects of tension are really in a favorable position when building quality of character and a solid character. Since they already fight a constant battle with negativity, their ability to see an issue coming and to modify their behavior can be used to their advantage. But, and this is a huge thing to understand. In any case, and this is a colossal thing to comprehend. You can't become involved with the pessimism. Instead, listen to your thoughts and find active, positive solutions going forward. This enables you to assume responsibility for your tension in a constructive design that makes a solid character.

How to Recognize Anxiety as a Problem?

As we have referenced previously, nervousness is typical to encounter occasionally. The general sentiment of apprehension or restlessness, for the most part, strikes individuals a couple of times throughout their life. At the point when tension starts to turn into an issue; however, it can influence your connections, your activity, and your satisfaction. The battle or flight pressure reaction is gainful to the most flagging threat.

You might be asking, when is anxiety reasonable and beneficial. There are a vast number of encounters in life that can cause ordinary anxiety in individuals. At the point when life presents a first of any kind, regardless of whether it is a date, the primary day of school, a new position, or an excursion tension and nerves will kick in. These extraordinary occasions may appear to be unimportant to you, yet any adjustment in what your brain seems to be ordinary or routine will trigger nervousness. This is normal, though, and can be beneficial. It is your mind's way of readying your body for potential danger and reminding you to be cautious of the newness. Normal nervousness sits back and can be overseen without an excess of reasonable ideas.

So when does anxiety become an issue? While you realize that typical degrees of anxiety are useful, raised, and delayed nervousness is an issue. The essential contrast between usual tension and issue nervousness in the force of the experience. Normal anxiety is intermittent and is based on certain events or situations that the person is experiencing. Problem anxiety is chronic, often irrational, and interferes with the person's normal life functions. If your anxiety is meddling with your life, if you are dodging circumstances, ending up stressing unremittingly, experiencing difficulty focusing, or having memory and judgment passes at that point, the chances are that your tension is an issue. For some, the symptoms are so intense and consuming that it begins to cause problems in their family lives, their work lives, and in their relationships. The effects of issue nervousness may incorporate heart palpitations, stomach issues, and other physical real reactions. These physical indications rationally make musings of extreme stress and social changes that change how you collaborate with others in your life. If issue nervousness is left unchecked and untreated, it might prompt tension issues, wrecked connections, and melancholy. When nervousness progresses to a tension issue seeing a specialist gets essential to work in consistently life. Nervousness attacks can become crippling whenever left unchecked. The most obvious signs of problem anxiety are;

• Often feel wild of their wellbeing and life

• Experience more significant levels of by and large pressure

• Often battle with low confidence.

• Feel apprehensive in numerous social circumstances

- Have trouble overseeing pressure

- Have better standards of themselves as well as other people

- Feel returned love is execution-based.

- Often have unfortunate limits.

- Are frequently compulsive workers

- Are all the more frequently debilitated

- Often have unfortunate connections.

- Become internal concentrated and harp on their wellbeing condition and individual issues

- Visit the specialist all the more frequently.

- Tax the therapeutic framework (with visit outings to their primary care physician or crisis rooms)

- Are bound to take meds

- Are bound to have other medical issues

- Are generally increasingly despondent

- Experience sporadic enthusiastic practices

- Often brisk to blow up.

- Regularly feel disrupted

- Regularly feel overpowered

- Feel disengaged or withdrew from the real world and life

- Often feel they are simply on the edge of losing control.

- Often aren't dependable (because their side effects may keep them from finishing)

- Become internal concentrated and harp on their wellbeing condition and individual issues

- May hop from relationship to relationship looking for flawlessness

- May hop from occupation to work as a result of more elevated levels of pressure

- Live a confined way of life (inside their willful "safe zones")

- Feel life is cruising them by

- Question their confidence

- Obsessive tallying and other interruption methods

If you are experiencing any of these side effects or your general nervousness has kept going longer than a half year, it is basic that you look for help from a medical expert and a therapist.

Chapter 3: Solutions for Anxiety in Relationships

Tension can be challenging to oversee. However, there are solutions, and when you are seeing someone, those solutions can be worked through altogether. Although some anxiety in a relationship is ordinary, having it rule your relationship can turn it harmful, regularly harming the individual you love most. For some people who suffer from anxiety, bouncing from relationship to relationship helps to ease their anxiety only for a short period, when insecurity creeps in again. They are regularly left inquiring as to why their connections consistently come up short, never entirely understanding that it is their anxiety that is pushing individuals away.

Studies have indicated that individuals with low confidence have far more elevated levels of insecurity, especially in their relationship. It keeps them from making a profound and significant association with their accomplices. Individuals with low confidence not just need their partner to see them in a superior light than they see themselves. Still, in moments of self-doubt, they experience difficulty, in any event, perceiving their accomplice's confirmations. Acting out their insecurities pushes their partner further away, creating a self-fulfilling prophecy, and because this struggle is internal and goes on most of the time, the anxiety compounds. It is essential to manage your weaknesses without involving your partner in them. You can do this by taking two steps:

⟨ Uncover the real roots of our insecurity.

⟨ Challenge your inner critic that sabotages our relationship.

You should set up where your uncertainty originates from regardless. Nothing stirs inaccessible damages like a cozy relationship and being open to somebody. Our connections work up old sentiments from our past more than all else. Our brains are even flooded with the same neurochemicals in both situations. Everyone has a working model for relationships that were formed in our early attachments to influential caretakers. Our first example can shape our grown-up connections. Your style of connection impacts which kind of accomplices we pick and the elements that happen in our relationships. A safe connection design encourages an individual to be progressively sure and aloof. At the point when somebody has an on edge or engrossed connection style, they might be bound to feel shaky toward their partner.

There is a mystery to overseeing and conquering the obstructions that reason you to experience the ill effects of your uneasiness. The secret is recognizing that the hindrances that scare you and make your negative musings are the way to carrying on with a reliable and secure life. When you grasp these impediments and choose to work through them, you will have the option to begin to build up more profound attention to where and when your frailties are originating from. The minute you start using your anxiety as a mindful reminder that your insecurities and mistrust are rearing their ugly head, you are better able to manage the consequences positively. Furthermore, here is the uplifting news; all frailties are an opportunity to benefit some work in bettering yourself. When you begin to focus, and you are never again determined by your uneasiness and your uncertainties, you will have the option to take a shot at some incredible strides to reinforce your relationship. These steps are;

They forgive your past

Since the more significant part of your insecurities has been formed by a family member or authority figure reprimanding you, recognize this and try to identify who they are. At that point, begin to excuse them gradually. Defend and comprehend that they were driven by their frailties, battling, and were in all likeliness battling with their very own evil spirits. People are not great, and given that they carry on incompletely, we as a whole do. This doesn't mean they were directly in what they did, but instead that you can comprehend, they also were battling through their very own fights. To forgive them for their bad behavior will be healing for you because holding on to resentment isn't helping you. When you go of the past, you can start to mend, slowly and carefully.

Acknowledge yourself, the great and the awful

Pause for a minute to respite and take a self-evaluation of your life and how you are living it. Notice the pieces of yourself, both your body and your internal identity, that you don't care for or might want to change. Presently, investigate these pieces of you, and attempt to imagine the love for yourself. Consider yourself to be a whole individual made up of large and flawed parts. Recognize that you are meriting love as an accomplice since everybody, paying little respect to their flaws, has the right to be adored. On the off chance that you are doing combating, attempt to imagine why you love your companions, in any event, realizing they are flawed. In the same manner, you love your companions; you should show love toward yourself.

Start to rehearse self-approval

Insecurity drives an individual to look for others' endorsements. If you see yourself needing another person's applause and consideration, attempt to stop for a minute and supplant that requirement for support with self-approval. When you remove the intensity of others' approval and begin to give your endorsement, you move the power of certainty working to yourself. Having another person's consent is decent to have; however, having your very own support is groundbreaking. Try not to misunderstand us; this doesn't mean you are dismissing or don't need association with others, or love from your partner. You can, in any case, be adored by your accomplice while additionally rehearsing self-approval.

Stop comparing yourself

Comparing yourself and what others look like, what they're doing, how fruitful they are, or the amount they have is never a significant correlation. This conduct effectively hurts you, so as opposed to getting desirous or contrasting yourself and another person, change your point of view. Understand that you are unique and comparing yourself with someone else is like trying to compare an apple with an orange. Attempt to be cheerful for them and happy in their prosperity, understanding that they are on an alternate way to you and that they also have their very own issues. When you wish everyone well and embrace the path you are on, you take away your anxiety's power over you and can be joyful for yourself and others. In all honesty, there is somebody who might be listening who is most likely contrasting themselves with you as well.

Figure out how to be trustful at the time

By using the devices in this book and rehearsing them, when nervousness raises its head as well as consistently, you will confide in yourself. At the point when you can create trust at the time that you can support, you can appreciate the minute without nervousness dominating. Figuring out how to be trustful at the time sets aside some effort to create. Recollect that figuring out how to believe yourself is indistinguishable to figuring out how to confide in another person. In any case, when you can tell in yourself and trust that you will know the distinction among tension and genuine indications of threat, you and your partner will have the option to start to appreciate each other's conversation again.

While strolling your way to mending and joy, you will consistently discover things that will incite your nervousness, yet the more mindful you become, and the more you practice the methods in this book, the simpler it will be to haul yourself out of full tension. Before long, you will end up getting all the more tolerating of yourself and your accomplice's love. Together you will have the option to fabricate your relationship to a reliable spot that both of you can appreciate without dread or hatred.

After perusing the parts above on connection type, you should realize your connection style. This is useful because it can assist you with achieving ways you might be reproducing a dynamic from quite a while ago. It can help you with choosing better accomplices and structure more advantageous connections, which can change your connection style. It can make you increasingly mindful of how your sentiments of frailty might be lost because of something old rather than our present relationship. By changing your connection type, you can battle tension with actual conduct and a caring, steady accomplice next to you.

Your weaknesses can likewise originate from the essential inward voice that you've disguised dependent on negative programming from quite a while ago. This inward pundit will, in general, be exceptionally vocal about the things that truly matter to you, similar to your connections. Connections challenge the center emotions you have about yourself and drive you out of your customary range of familiarity. They drive up the volume of your inner voice and reopen unresolved wounds from our past. If you are already negative or have a tendency to be self-critical, relationships will amplify your anxiety, often forcing negativity to the surface.

Here is a recap of how to deal with your tension in your relationship through every situation and help you in recuperating and pushing ahead.

• **Think about what is causing your jealousy** – You can think about what sentiments, individuals, and sensations cause you to get desirous and flood your brain with envious musings. Is what you are feeling connected to a past occasion? Perhaps it a family relationship or an existing negative perception from your childhood. When you can associate your feelings and eruptions to the things that occurred in your past, you will have a more precise way on the most proficient method to work through those feelings in the present.

• **Remain vulnerable and stay calm in the present**– It doesn't make a difference how envious you are, there is continuously an approach to discover your way back to your actual self and to mollify your viewpoint. This should be possible by tolerating that you are human and by managing your sentiments mercifully. Recall that desire and tension travels every which way in waves; they will step by step construct and die down after some time. You can acknowledge your envy and recognize your sentiments without responding to it. Learning devices that assist you with working through your jealousy without overcompensating. Alleviating breaths and long strolls are only a portion of the strategies that will help you with calming yourself. Recall that it is simpler to quiet down when you do not endure or tune in to the negative words and thoughts that originate from your inward critic. Getting the hang of quieting procedures can be troublesome; however, it is a theoretical apparatus to assist you with facing your essential musings.

• **Stop acting out** – The internal voice that makes you blow up and guide you to lash out at your accomplice and companions cause long haul harm in your connections. If you allow it to spiral out of control and you are stuck in a look of jealousy, it may even wreck your relationship. This is a form of self-sabotage because jealousy causes you to lash out or punish someone you care for without it being their fault. This is particularly valid for individuals in a relationship. At the point when you do this, you are making the very situation you are generally scared of. You may wind up harming and undermining your accomplice, which disregards their adoration for you. This thus will intensify your sentiments of doubt and the dread that they will leave you. You may accidentally urge them to follow up on your conduct, making them become deterred from you, concealing their emotions or their activities to dodge your doubt and jealousy.

• **Find security in yourself** – Focusing on yourself and finding your very own feeling of self-security is the best thing you can accomplish for sentiments of jealousy that trigger nervousness. It may not be simple yet by taking every necessary step to quiet the pundit inside you and persuade yourself that you will be alright, regardless of whether that implies being without anyone else is fundamental. The acknowledgment that you needn't bother with one explicit individual to adore you to entire and glad is enabling. Individuals usually are imperfect and have restrictions, and understanding that one individual can't give you everything that you need continually is significant. At the point when you practice sympathy with yourself, you can face the essential voice inside and your negative thoughts. You don't have to close individuals out or disconnect yourself from the world to have the option to be sympathetic to yourself. What is means that you grasp your life, your blemishes, and your deficiencies totally, realizing that you are sufficiently able to defeat challenges and disappointments. Recollect that the main thing you can control in life is how you respond to your conditions. Decide to respond entirely.

• **Don't stop being competitive** – While a few people don't care for being focused, it is excellent whenever done effectively. Being aggressive doesn't mean you are deciding to be the best at something. It implies you can set a sensible objective and state that you are giving your best to have the option to accomplish it. At the point when you are focused on yourself, you are grasping everything that will assist you with positively achieving your objectives. Rather than being envious, harmful, and lashing out, you can move and interface with the best characteristics in you. When you have associated with your internal identity, you will have the option to find a way to carry you closer to your objectives. Regard is earned, not naturally offered, and to win that regard, you should be chivalrous in your activities and aware of the ramifications for those activities.

Moreover, if you need to feel adored and acknowledged reliably by your partner, you should be cherishing and make them feel esteemed in your relationship as well. When you are predictable in your need to act with honesty and to effectively seek after your objectives, you can win the fight against tension that is brought about by envy and begin to become yourself again. Somebody independent from any other person and novel.

• **Don't shy away from talking about it** – When desire starts to assume control over it gets significant for you to locate the suitable individual to discuss your sentiments in a manner that is sound for you to express precisely how you feel. These individuals are the ones who bolster your positive attributes and who help you not to lose all sense of direction in your negative thoughts or spiraling into desire. Everybody has companions who blow up or get stirred up when certain subjects are examined, and we are not saying they shouldn't be your companions.

However, they are not the individuals you should converse with when you feel envious or on edge. These individuals will most likely make you feel increasingly on side or desirous before the finish of the discussion. As a result of this, you should search out individuals who won't just help you yet will assist you with thinking soundly about the circumstance. At the point when you are addressing these individuals, make sure to recognize to yourself that your negative musings are nonsensical and that your sentiments are not right. This causes you to alleviate feelings of desire because the sounding load up enables you to listen to your musings noisy, helping you to change your activities and how you would respond. If excitement turns out to be an excess of you should discover help from a specialist who can assist you with understanding how you are feeling, how to deal with those emotions, and work through the foundation of where your sentiments of envy are originating from.

Reconnect with your partner;

Connect with your partner consistently; as your relationship develops, you and your accomplice will turn out to be less eager to get to know one another.

Require some investment consistently to invest some energy alone together, sitting idle, however speaking and looking at nothing significant.

Reconnect the physical closeness; Intimate and passionate associations are solidly connected, and dismissing one can hurt the other. You don't really should have additional time doing it, however guaranteeing that you are both having the sort of personal connection that you need is one method for extending passionate bonds.

Practice compassionate tuning in.

Become solid as a part of your character by;

Tune in before talking.

Tolerating recognition and giving applause where it is expected.

Rehearsing positive, open non-verbal communication.

I understand that activities express stronger than words.

Working with a therapist to get past your uneasiness and finding the correct answers to facilitate your manifestations and refocus will mend you as well as your relationship. A portion of the things you can do at home to help battle your uneasiness is;

• **Exercise** – It is imperative to see how activity impacts the body as well as the mind too. Daily use is essential in the individual life. At the point when you practice regularly, your account discharges endorphins into your circulatory system, which improves your mind-set. Also, your psyche is occupied from your restless musings. Practicing has been deductively to help your general state of mind and decrease the indications of nervousness and sadness. As physical exercise increments, so makes the improvement of your anxiety. A few activities to take an interest in that have been explicitly connected to assisting with tension are yoga and judo. This is because these activities for an individual to be careful in their developments and center while clearing their brain. As you structure an everyday practice with your activity, your body will start to deliver serotonin and endorphins previously, during, and after exercise. These synthetic concoctions that are provided in mind are appeared to diminish melancholy and uneasiness fundamentally. Training supports confidence, improves certainty, enables you to start to feel engaged and reliable, and causes you to manufacture solid and new social connections and companionship.

• **Begin a healthy diet** – The mind requires an enormous measure of vitality and sustenance to work effectively. Healthy nutrition can bring enormous changes in your physical health. A terrible eating regimen implies that you are not providing the supplements that are required for your mind's synapses to work effectively. In light of that, it might be worsening the manifestations of your nervousness. By eating a sound eating regimen and filling your plate with entire and new nourishment, drinking the perfect measure of water and guaranteeing that you are taking in the correct nutrients, minerals, and trans fats day by day, you are giving your cerebrum the proper nourishment to capacity and battle anxiety. A solid eating routine likewise implies dealing with your gut and stomach related tract. Recollect that a sound eating routine methods removing improved beverages like frosted teas, soft drinks, and prepared natural product juices. Studies have demonstrated that individuals who drink over the top measure of pop each day are over 30% bound to experience the ill effects of nervousness and melancholy than the individuals who don't. Unsweetened beverages like plain espresso, homegrown teas, and water that has the organic product in it are a far more beneficial alternative when keeping your body and cerebrum hydrated. Caffeine is likewise a supporter of tension side effects and ought to be curtailed to battle the symptoms of caffeine.

No more liquor – liquor is a focal sensory system depressant and is a known reason for tension as we all know that it is very harmful to our health. A few people do attempt to dull the impacts of their nervousness by drinking liquor; however, actually, liquor is regularly the base of your tension. Liquor intrudes on rest, gets dried out the body, and occupies an individual from managing the current issues as opposed to going up against and recognizing the root and reason for their anxiety.

• **Catch up on your rest** – Bad dozing propensities affect an individual's state of mind. This is because the mind's synapses need time to rest and recharge to keep the body's mind-set steady. Legitimate, eternal rest enables the cerebrum to adjust hormone levels and allows an individual to all the more likely to adapt to their anxiety. Unfortunate dozing propensities and sleep deprivation needn't bother with synthetic compounds to be amended. Awful resting propensities can be rectified utilizing standard techniques including melatonin, teas, homegrown mixes, exercise, and contemplation. At the point when you ensure that you are getting high, quality rest, your mind will start to address its hormone levels.

• **Begin to address your feelings**– This book covers dealing with your negative contemplations and frames of mind broadly, and being restless miracles the body's hormones and powers the brain to create more synthetic concoctions to attempt to feel upbeat. In the end, the cerebrum gets exhausted and can't deliver the hormones expected to battle sickness and tension. Via preparing your psyche to consider reflection emphatically and care thoroughly, you can change your recognition on what's going on and start to assume responsibility for your negative considerations. By battling and hushing your very own negative contemplations, you can work through your nervousness, ensuring that you are better ready to recuperate in your relationship. Make sure to rehearse all types of positive confirmation, which incorporates excusing yourself, appreciation for your life, and consideration to other people. At the point when you can get positive, uneasiness begins to slow, and you are better ready to speak with your accomplice without negative, foolish conduct subverting you. Continuously recollect that you are responsible for your own life. If there are circumstances that are making your tension erupt, you can transform them.

• **Reduce your pressure** – Stress builds nervousness higher than ever and triggers the body's battle or flight reaction. By learning techniques to manage pressure and control, focusing on factors you are enabling your body to all the more likely deal with its normal reactions to what it sees as a risk. By learning techniques, you would be able to handle the immense pressure. Distinguishing what makes worry for you enables you to either remove the pressure or create methodologies to assist you with dealing with your pressure. Rehearsing unwinding systems, setting aside effort for yourself to revive, and appreciating life is large approaches to loosen up your mind and enable nervousness to ease. Become flexible to stress and realize that, by and by, you have power overpressure.

• **Reach out and locate a solid help base** – A stable relationship begins with solid fellowships. Having a decent informal organization that offers you support and a sounding board as you work through your tension is critical to mending. Uneasiness can make an individual need to detach themselves; however, a decent help structure implies you will consistently have somebody to connect with when tension backs its head. These ought to be individuals who locate the positive in you and can give you sensible and objective reactions when you talk about what is causing your uneasiness. They should provoke you to investigate inside and should assist you with quieting your inward pundit. Ensure that you keep great, quality contact with your loved ones who make you like yourself. Do whatever it takes not to become involved with others' pessimism. Attempt to volunteer to increase point of view in your life and associate with other people who have emotional wellness issues. On the off chance that you are not yet at the point where you need to see an advisor, attempt to join a care group. Consider embracing and creature to help sooth your nervousness and show you, unqualified love.

- **Find your motivation** – People who have a solid feeling of their motivation can deal with pressure and nervousness superior to anything the individuals who don't. Finding your motivation gives you a boundary against the impediments your internal pundit outlines for you. Those with a solid feeling of direction will, in general, discover life all the more satisfying and can see the positive qualities in each circumstance instead of stressing over what terrible may occur. Your motivation doesn't really need to be a vocation or a leisure activity; finding your otherworldliness, investing energy considering what your qualities are, volunteering at covers or no benefit associations, recognizing and utilizing your one of a kind gifts to help other people and recognizing that life is about rhythmic movement are for the most part methods for finding your motivation. At the point when you discover your motivation, you can get strong and fair with yourself, which enables you to be straightforward with your accomplice also.

Utilizing a few or the entirety of the systems set above is the way to defeating nervousness in your relationship. Dealing with your tension is not just about looking for treatment. It is discovering answers for a deal with your degrees of uneasiness such that it works for you and eventually your accomplice. By understanding that your accomplice isn't your advisor and assuming liability for your tension, you will be better ready to work through the central issues that have made your nervousness in any case. At the point when you comprehend these center issues, you start to assume responsibility for your life again by working through your unreasonable and basic musings and supplanting them with positive contemplations and activities. Even though tension can never be relieved, it unquestionably can be made to do with procedures and way of life changes. Having the option to quietness your inward pundit, addressing your accomplice, enabling them to speak to tune in to them, and way of life changes all will allow you. Strengthening encourages you to assume responsibility for your life again and improve your relationship. On the off chance that you are involved with somebody who experiences nervousness, we believe that this book has helped you to all the more likely comprehend what tension is, the thing that drives uneasiness, and how to assist your cooperate with healing and deal with their tension. For the individuals who are enduring uneasiness, we trust that by perusing this book, you have had the option to enable yourself and make the strides that are expected to start improving your satisfaction and your relationship. Thus, assuming liability for your tension and choosing to work through it, utilizing a few or the entirety of the procedures in this book will enable you to tailor-make your adventure in recuperating yourself

and your relationship.

CONCLUSION

Anxiety can feel like an additional individual in the relation-ship, an irritating element that pushes among you and your accomplice. The tension appears to perpetuate uncertainty and disarray in the relationship continually. No one is set up for this in a relationship, yet you can't pick who you love, and there are no classes you can take to more readily set you up for adoring somebody with a psychological wellness issue. However, that nervousness doesn't need to obliterate or put weight on a relationship. When an individual figure out how to get tension and how it can influence the two accomplices and the relationship in general, the relationship can be recu-perated, enabling the two partners to interface all the more profoundly on a passionate level. Regardless of whether you are telling your accomplice that you experience the ill effects of nervousness, or getting some information about their ten-sion, how the subject is examined can represent the moment of truth a relationship. Individuals who experience the ill ef-fects of nervousness invested a great deal of their energy stressing and envisioning situations in which everything without exception could turn out badly.

They over examine their connections, posing negative inquiries, and enabling the responses to reflect terrible results. While it is typical for individuals to have these sorts of considerations and questions now and again, nervousness intensifies them. Those with a tension issue consider these inquiries regularly and with power. Individuals with anxiety envision the direst outcome imaginable, enabling their psyches to assume control over their sound point of view. On edge musings at that point cause physiological manifestations in the body. Uneasiness doesn't just influence the individual experiencing it. It can put anxiety on your accomplice and can pulverize a relationship.

Tension doesn't have to risk your relationship. At the point when you overcome your feelings and utilize the correct adapting systems, you can have a healthy relationship. These adapting systems will prevent uneasiness from also causing anxiety in your relationship. The duty regarding assuming responsibility for your feelings lies with you as the uneasiness sufferer. You are seeing a specialist who can show you solid methods for dealing with stress that will improve your satisfaction in and outside of your relationship. On the off chance that you are in a long haul submitted relationship, you may consider heading off to a couple of couple's sessions to work through any nervousness gives that are situated in your relationship. By doing this, you are easing the heat off of your accomplice and your relationship.

At the point when you have negative musings, anxiety takes steps to crush you and makes them cry that your life is loaded with misfortune. Be that as it may, the fact of the matter is your very own negative musings make you the cause of all your problems. At the point when you enable yourself to enjoy negative thoughts, you are making your misfortune. You have to turn out to be increasingly mindful again and hear the words as you express them to yourself to sift through the pessimism. When you can perceive the negative words and thoughts, you can stop and counter them with positive or elective messages. By being certain and hopeful you can transform antagonism into truth, not fear.

Because things haven't turned out in different connections or you have been frustrated in the past doesn't imply that they won't be diverse this time. Pessimism doesn't need to be something you are tormented with until the end of time. You are the ace of your destiny, and when you change pessimism to energy, all of you, your hopeful standpoint to radiate through into your relationship.

Another issue that stems from low confidence and nervousness is desire. Desire can assume control over your life if you don't take a few to get back some composure on it and it can overwhelm you, It can be a terrifying feeling to feel. It can frequently destroy connections and propagate a negative idea. At the point when you enable envy to overwhelm you or to shape how you think about yourself or your accomplice, you are conceivably disrupting your relationship. By attempting to comprehend where your envious sentiments are originating from, figuring out how to manage them, and discovering approaches to adjust to your feelings, you are allowing your relationship to thrive. The individuals who experience the ill effects of uneasiness know about these dangerous musings experiencing your psyche, yet envy starts to frame when these thoughts begin to get fanatical.

The main problem comes in when those with uneasiness will, in general, retreat trying to shield themselves from the envisioned risk or torment that they believe is happening. Be that as it may, the more you retreat, the more removed your accomplice will become, and the more envious you will turn into. By effectively chipping away at your nervousness and your jealous sentiments, you are making your relationship a need and deciding to love and close with your accomplice rather than desirous and unreliable. At the point when you choose to battle desire, you are intentionally telling your accomplice that you have a sense of security and secure enoug

in yourself and them to place your trust in your relationship.

The most well-known indications of a relationship in a diff

cult situation are how the accomplices differ or battle wit

one another and how they settle the contention betwee

them. Their goals, whether negative or positive, can influ

ence the tone of the relationship and how clashes are taken

care of later on. Contradictions that form into petty squab

bling or on edge consistent clash, as a rule, end up in a more

uncertain possibility of the relationship enduring. Fortunate

ly, there are arrangements, and settling strife can be moder

ately simple with the assistance of a specialist. On the off

chance that you and your accomplice are not yet and the

purpose of seeing a therapist, rehearsing sympathy without

judgment will go far in settling strife. Sympathetic tuning in

and proclamations should be possible by telling your accom-

plice that you are tuning in. Since individuals you experience

the ill effects of tension are commonly centered around

themselves, they will, in general, contend such that makes

them like themselves. At the point when individual practices compassionate tuning in and correspondence, they guarantee that their accomplice realizes that they are being tuned in to. Fortunately, it gets considerably more straightforward.

While building a compassionate proclamation, one should utilize, "So you feel that...." This maintains the emphasis on your accomplice and away from your sentiments of uneasiness. At the point when the two accomplices utilize this system to listen cautiously to the passionate needs of their life partner, it stays away from strife and addresses the more profound issues close by.

A specific degree of anxiety is something to be thankful for and inquire about shows that great pressure can inspire and energize an individual in their lives. Nervousness can be only the admonition sign. You have to carry attention to your present circumstance and roll out some important improvements throughout your life. Consistent stress and anxiety can be a sign that a few parts of your life are off track an need altering. Even though your nervousness indications ca be hard to oversee, by setting aside some effort to investigat and taking a shot at adapting to your uneasiness, it very wel may be a genuine open door for self-development. Wheneve tension strikes, think about what message it has for you anc the potential changes you may need to make in your life. A: opposed to continually being viewed as an obstruction, tension may assist you with feeling progressively inspired and arranged when looked with difficulties.

Anxiety doesn't have to control your life or wreck your relationship. It very well may be utilized to fabricate a solid character and help with building up an impressive, regarded character. A solid character doesn't mean you should be boisterous, scary, or over the top to show your character. It is conceivable to have a solid character in calm certainty too. Uneasiness has its favorable circumstances. It sends a sign to the body that something is significant or could represent a peril to you. Having uneasiness about your accomplice shoes that you care for them on a more profound level, if you didn't encounter nervousness, you would most likely, at some point or another, find that you couldn't care less as profoundly as you suspected for your accomplice.

Intense tension should be abolished, however, particularly if you will probably push ahead into an important association with your accomplice. Although nervousness can't be relieved, it unquestionably can be controlled, and you as the tension sufferer have a decision in whether you decided to participate in your very own negative conduct. Nervousness builds inspiration, reason, and your satisfaction to a limited degree. Truly, we concur that it can feel dreadful, yet outfit effectively, nervousness can feature regions in our lives that we have to investigate. It urges us to roll out the improvements we have to make to carry on with a more joyful, increasingly happy life.

Take control of your anxiety today. Build a more grounded

relationship and be a superior you!

FINAL WORDS

Thank you again for purchasing this book!

We really hope this book is able to help you.

The next step is for you to **join our email newsletter** to receive updates on any upcoming new book releases or promotions. You can sign-up for free and as a bonus, you will also receive our "*7 Fitness Mistakes You Don't Know You're Making*" book! This bonus book breaks down many of the most common fitness mistakes and will demystify many of the complexities and science of getting into shape. Having all this fitness knowledge and science organized into an actionable step-by-step book will help you get started in the right direction in your fitness journey! To join our free email newsletter and grab your free book, please visit the link and signup: **www.effingopublishing.com/gift**

Finally, if you enjoyed this book, then we would like to ask you for a favor, would you be kind enough to leave a review for this book? It would be greatly appreciated! Thank yo

and good luck in your journey!

ABOUT THE CO-AUTHORS

Our name is Alex & George Kaplo; we're both certified personal trainers from Montreal, Canada. Will start off by saying we are not the biggest guys you will ever meet and this has never really been our goal. In fact, we started working out to overcome our biggest insecurity when we were younger, which was our self-confidence. You may be going through some challenges right now, or you may simply want to get fit, and we can certainly relate.

For us personally, we always kind were interested in the

health & fitness world and wanted to gain some muscle due to the numerous bullying in our teenage years. We figured we can do something about how our body looks like. This was the beginning of our transformation journey. We had no idea where to start, but we both just got started. We felt worried and afraid at times that other people would make fun of us for doing the exercises the wrong way. We always wished we had a friend to guide us and who could just show us the ropes.

After a lot of work, studying and countless trial and errors. Some people began to notice how we were both getting more fit and how we were starting to form a keen interest in the topic. This led many friends and new faces to come to us and ask us for fitness advice. At first, it seemed odd when people asked us to help them get in shape. But what kept us going is when they started to see changes in their own body and told us it's the first time that they saw real results! From there, more people kept coming to us, and it made both of us realize after so much reading and studying in this field that it did help us but it also allowed us to help others. To date, we have coached and trained numerous clients who have achieved some pretty amazing results.

Today, both of us own & operate this publishing business, where we bring passionate and expert authors to write about health and fitness topics. We also run an online fitness business and we would love to connect with you by inviting you to visit the website on the following page and signing up to our e-mail newsletter (you will even get a free book).

Last but not least, if you are in the position we were once in and you want some guidance, don't hesitate and ask... will be there to help you out!

Your coaches,

Alex & George Kaplo

Download another book for Free

We want to thank you for purchasing this book and offer you another book (just as long and valuable as this book "Health & Fitness Mistakes You Don't Know You're Making" completely free.

Visit the link below to signup and receive it:

www.effingopublishing.com/gift

In this book, we will break down the most common health & fitness mistakes, you are probably committing right now and will reveal how you can easily get in the best shape of your life!

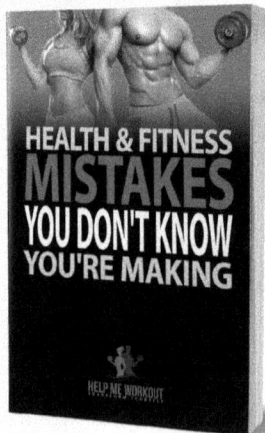

In addition to this valuable gift, you will also have an opportunity to get our new books for free, enter giveaways, and receive other valuable emails from us. Again, visit the link to sign up:

www.effingopublishing.com/gift

The information herein is offered for informational purposes solely, and universal as so. The presentation of the information is without contract any type of guarantee assurance.

The trademarks that are used are without any consent, and the publicatic of the trademark is without permission or backing by the trademark own er. All trademarks and brands within this book are for clarifying purpose only and are the owned by the owners themselves, not affiliated with thi document.

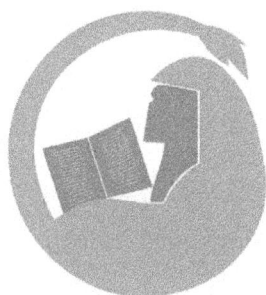

EFFINGO
Publishing

For more great books visit:

<u>EffingoPublishing.com</u>

www.ingramcontent.com/pod-product-compliance
Lightning Source LLC
Chambersburg PA
CBHW050737030426
42336CB00012B/1613